GIANTS OF THE OLD TESTAMENT

LESSONS ON LIVING FROM

MOSES

Living in the Valleys

A devotional by

WOODROW KROLL

BACK TO THE BIBLE®
Lincoln, Nebraska

CONTENTS

DAY 1

Exodus 15:21-22

And Miriam answered them: "Sing to the LORD, for He has triumphed gloriously! The horse and its rider He has thrown into the sea!" So Moses brought Israel from the Red Sea; then they went out into the Wilderness of Shur. And they went three days in the wilderness and found no water.

Living in the Valleys

Mountaintops are great places. As you stand on some lofty peak it seems as if you can see forever. But most people don't live on mountains. The demands of reality require that life is generally lived in the valleys.

The Israelites had just come through one of the high points of their nation's history—a mountaintop experience. Pursued by Pharaoh's army, they crossed the Red Sea with dry sandals and then saw the waters rush together again upon their enemy's horses and chariots. With tremendous joy, they sang God's praise. Then they hit the valley—from the fresh air of the mountaintop to the dry, oppressive air of the wilderness. For three days they traveled without finding water. Compared to the mountaintops, the valleys are real spiritual challenges.

But that's the way real life is. Spiritual mountaintops are wonderful. You feel particularly close to God during your devotional time; you return from a weekend retreat knowing the living Lord has met with you in a special way; you come home from church after the pastor's sermon has met a deep spiritual need in your life. You revel in the warmth of these marvelous mountaintop experiences.

But that's not where you live. You live in the valley, where there are dirty dishes to wash, lawns to mow and children to raise. Often real life isn't much fun.

Fortunately, Israel discovered, as will you, that God is with you both on the mountain and in the valley. He never leaves you, never allows you out of His loving care. We all appreciate those times when we encounter God in a special way, but we know that God is also with us when we sink to spiritual lows and feel a little dry. The God you meet in the good times is the same God who meets you in the hard times.

The God who dwells on the mountains also inhabits the valleys.

Reflections/Prayer Requests

_____

_____

_____

DAY 2

Exodus 15:23

Now when they came to Marah, they could not drink the waters of Marah, for they were bitter. Therefore the name of it was called Marah.

By the Waters of Bitterness

During the last few decades the news has been filled with stories about a pollutant called acid rain. It's an increasing problem in the northeastern United States and Canada. Acid rain is the result of sulfur and nitrogen oxides being washed from the air by normal rainfall. These pollutants are killing whole forests and destroying fish and other aquatic life in numerous lakes.

The people of Israel encountered a similar situation at an oasis they called Marah, which means "bitter." Something had so polluted the water that it was undrinkable. The people of God were in danger of dying of thirst. But when we need God most, He is always there. Jehovah directed Moses to a tree that miraculously restored the pureness of the water when cast into it (v. 25).

Bitter water also can destroy our spiritual lives. James asks, "Does a spring send forth fresh water and bitter from the same opening?" (James 3:11). The sweet spirit God wants for us cannot exist in a heart polluted by bitterness. Bitterness on the inside will eventually manifest itself on the outside. No matter how carefully we think we have concealed it, bitterness will contaminate all we are, all we say, and all we do. The only solution is to apply the healing balm of God's Spirit to the bitterness of our lives.

If you are being polluted by bitterness, isn't it time for God's freshness? Confess that your bitterness is a sin that is keeping you miserably distant from God. Ask for His forgiveness and begin to enjoy a renewed sweetness.

A bitter spirit will keep you from being a better person.

Reflections/Prayer Requests

_____

_____

_____

_____

_____

_____

_____

_____

_____

DAY 3

Exodus 15:24

And the people murmured against Moses, saying, "What shall we drink?"

The Attitude of Ingratitude

Hot springs and cold springs are found side by side in some parts of Mexico. Because of the convenience of this natural phenomenon, women often bring their laundry to such places so they can boil their clothes in the hot springs and then rinse them in the cold ones. A tourist who was watching this procedure commented to his Mexican guide, "I imagine they think Mother Nature is pretty generous to supply such ample, clean, hot and cold water here side by side for their free use." The guide replied, "No, Señor, there is much grumbling because she supplies no soap."

Ingratitude is not limited to Mexican peasants; Israel demonstrated the same attitude. God had just performed some awe-inspiring miracles for His people's benefit. He had slain the first born of Egypt so that Pharaoh would free the Israelites. He had provided a pillar of cloud by day and a pillar of fire at night to guide their journey. He had opened the Red Sea for them to cross and brought it crashing back on the Egyptian army pursuing them. Yet when they hit their first snag, instead of trusting God, they turned to complaining.

8

Times of need are times for praying, not complaining. Complaining says to God, "You aren't taking very good care of me." Prayer says to God, "I may not understand what's happening, but I trust You to take care of me."

Do you feel life is treating you unfairly? Are you tempted to complain? Try this. Take a notebook and list some of the marvelous things God has already done in your life, such as providing your salvation, a measure of health, a supportive family and an inspired Bible. Then look with confidence that He will provide for your situation today as well.

Nothing cures ingratitude as quickly as a good memory.

Reflections/Prayer Requests

_____

_____

_____

_____

_____

_____

_____

_____

_____

_____

DAY 4

Exodus 15:25

*So he cried out to the L*ORD*, and the L*ORD*
showed him a tree; and when he cast it into the
waters, the waters were made sweet. There He
made a statute and an ordinance for them.*

Cry Out

On a gloomy day in 1857, a man in New
York City, Jeremiah Lanthier, scanned the
morning newspaper. He was distressed to
read that the depression gripping the nation
was causing fear and panic among the people. Factories were closing and thousands
were unemployed. Although Lanthier didn't
know what to do, he knew who did! That day
he sent a note to all his business acquain-
tances, telling them that at noon a prayer
meeting would be held in his office.

On the first day no one came. All alone he
prayed fervently that God would bring about
a great change in him and in America. The
second day a few friends joined him. A short
time later similar gatherings were started
around the city. Then like wildfire, the movement spread to all parts of the country. Some
historians say that this effort of united prayer
and faith was an integral part of the improve-
ment in the economy that soon followed.

Moses also faced a situation for which he had no answers, but he knew who did. Fervently he cried out to God, and God showed him what to do. It was not something he would have dreamed up on his own; it was better. The waters of Marah were bitter, and so were God's people about the quality of the water. The Israelites grumbled about many little things, but this was life-threatening. All Moses could do was pray to God and trust His answer, regardless of how unorthodox that answer may be.

What do you do when you don't know what to do? Follow the example set by other godly people—cry out to the Lord and He will answer. If you are willing to follow His instructions, you will never be left without the right answers.

It's not what you know but who you know that counts.

Reflections/Prayer Requests

_____

_____

_____

_____

_____

DAY 5

Exodus 15:26

"If you diligently heed the voice of the LORD your God and do what is right in His sight, give ear to His commandments and keep all His statutes, I will put none of the diseases on you which I have brought on the Egyptians. For I am the LORD who heals you."

The Key to Health

Millions of people are exploring alternatives to traditional Western medicine. Such approaches as biofeedback, autogenics training, kenesiology, bioenergetics, reflexology, stress management, homeopathy, naturopathy and macrobiotics are just a few of the possibilities. But God offers the real key to health; it's called obedience.

God told the Israelites if they would "give ear to His commandments" and "keep all His statutes," they would avoid many of the illnesses that plagued the people of Egypt. This was not a matter of "buying" their obedience; it was a matter of natural consequences. By avoiding sin, they would avoid the unhealthy results of sin as well.

This principle still holds true today. We talk a great deal about breaking God's laws, but we really only break ourselves against God's laws. By living contrary to God's commandments, people contract sexually transmitted diseases; others weaken their bodies by a lack of exercise, poor diets and high stress; still others smoke or drink themselves into life-threatening danger.

It is God's will that you treat your body as the temple of the Holy Spirit (1 Cor. 6:19). Don't take it anywhere or expose it to anything that you know to be contrary to God's law. Get appropriate rest, eat healthy food and reduce stress. Obedience is the key. Living in harmony with His commandments will avoid many illnesses and make others more easy to overcome.

An ounce of obedience is worth a pound of protection.

Reflections/Prayer Requests

DAY 6

Does Jesus Care?

Almost a hundred years ago, a minister was plagued with ongoing trials and discouragements. When he thought he no longer could stand it, Rev. Frank Graeff remembered 1 Peter 5:7, which says, "casting all your care upon Him, for He cares for you." A new joy and peace encouraged his soul and he penned a song in which every stanza began with the question, "Does Jesus care . . . ?" The refrain echoes back, "O yes, He cares—I know He cares! His heart is touched with my grief."

The Israelites had reached a point in their journey where they were asking, "Does God care?" There had been years of hardship in Egypt. Then there was the hard trek through the wilderness. Finally they came upon a campsite where the water was unfit to drink. Life was not easy, but at last God brought them to Elim, where the water was plenteous and the trees were lush and shady. In the midst of their adversity, God brought them to a place of relief.

Does God care about you? He really does. If you're going through a tough time, don't give up. God has an Elim in your future. Scripture promises that God "will not allow you to be tempted [tried] beyond what you are able" (1 Cor. 10:13). Ahead, at God's rest stop, there is rest for the weary and tranquility for the distressed. If you're at Marah, the water of bitterness, look ahead to Elim, the place of peace.

In His time, God gives us rest from every test.

Reflections/Prayer Requests

_____

_____

_____

_____

_____

_____

_____

_____

_____

_____

DAY 7

Exodus 16:2-3

*Then the whole congregation of the children of Israel murmured against Moses and Aaron in the wilderness. And the children of Israel said to them, "Oh, that we had died by the hand of the L*ORD *in the land of Egypt, when we sat by the pots of meat and when we ate bread to the full! For you have brought us out into this wilderness to kill this whole assembly with hunger."*

Selective Memories

It's amazing how we are able to pick and choose the things we want to remember. A young boy was confronted by his father about the poor grades on his report card. "It's not my fault, Dad. I can't remember anything." "Well," his father assured him, "you're not going to any more baseball games until you get your grades up. And to begin with, forget tonight's game." "Wait a minute," said the boy. "You can't do that to me. The Braves are in town and Maddux is pitching. He was 15-11 last year with a 2.72 earned run average. He won four consecutive Cy Young awards and seven straight Gold Gloves. He led the league in ERA for three straight seasons, has been on five All-Star teams, and has won at least 15 games each of the last nine years."

Israel had the same problem—a selective memory. After only a short time in the wilderness, they had forgotten how they were required to make bricks without straw, how they had been beaten by merciless taskmasters and how the midwives were commanded to kill the infant Israelite boys to appease Pharaoh's fears. Instead, they remembered only the pots of meat and the loaves of bread they had enjoyed.

Satan may be tempting you in the same way. Maybe this new life is more difficult than you expected and your days as an unbeliever, as your now remember them, are looking pretty good after all. Perhaps the devil is reminding you of the sinful things you enjoyed in your old life and blocking the memories of despair and emptiness you felt as an unbeliever. Ask God to cut through these selective memories and help you recall the reality of the past. Don't be fooled by Satan's selective memories.

The memories Satan selects never reflect the way it really was.

Reflections/Prayer Requests

DAY 8

Exodus 16:4

*Then the L*ORD *said to Moses, "Behold, I will rain bread from heaven for you. And the people shall go out and gather a certain quota every day, that I may test them, whether they will walk in My law or not."*

Tested by the Blessings

Many tests come in the guise of hardship, illness or some other unpleasant experience—but not all of them. The good times can be just as much a test as the bad times.

When the people of Israel reached the Wilderness of Sin, they were unable to find food. This hot, barren wasteland offered nothing that would sustain a multitude of people. But God used this experience to test His children and teach them to trust Him. He graciously supplied a heavenly food that looked like a dewdrop, which the people called "manna." This miraculous gift was more than just a blessing, however. It was also God's test to see whether they would walk in His law or not.

Being obedient in the midst of plenteous blessings is often more difficult than when we are experiencing a multitude of difficulties. Pleasures can easily dull our spiritual ears so we no longer hear the Lord saying, "This is the way, walk in it" (Isa. 30:21). A lack of trials lulls us into a false sense of security and leaves us vulnerable to the attacks of Satan. It's no wonder that some people claim it's easier to survive poverty than wealth. Agur, the writer of Proverbs 30 prayed, "Feed me with the food You prescribe for me; lest I be full and deny You, and say, 'Who is the LORD?'" (vv. 8-9).

If you are experiencing a time of blessing, that's wonderful—but be sensitive to the potential for danger. Testing doesn't stop just because the trials have ceased. The need for obedience is constant whether the sun shines or not.

Trust and obey—every day.

Reflections/Prayer Requests

_____

_____

_____

_____

_____

_____

_____

_____

DAY 9

Exodus 16:7

And in the morning you shall see the glory of the LORD.

Glory in the Morning

Some days make you wonder if you should have stayed in bed. You cut yourself shaving, you spill coffee on your clothes, you have a computer crash at work, you receive overdue notices in the mail, and your son breaks his arm on the jungle gym at school. It's enough to make you want to crawl under the covers and hide.

The Israelites also were experiencing difficulties. They were hot, tired, hungry and upset. They even wondered if they should have stayed in Egypt. This trip was more difficult than they thought it was going to be.

In the midst of these trials, God did two things: He gave them manna for their physical bodies, but He also promised to reveal His glory to them "in the morning" for their spiritual well-being. God knew that the trials of the day needed a spiritual response as well as physical relief. And He chose to meet that spiritual need while the day was yet young.

When the day is hectic, the frustrations plentiful and the disappointments thick, it's time to turn to God. Yet how different the day might have gone had we turned to the Lord before we ever got started. Whether the events of the day change or not, when we have first spent time fellowshipping with God, we are better prepared to face them.

Perhaps you aren't a morning person—many people aren't. Yet getting up even 10 minutes earlier and spending those moments reading your Bible and praying will yield greater dividends than you might imagine. When you meet with God first in the morning, it's much easier to keep Him first all day.

How you begin your day will frequently determine how you end it.

Reflections/Prayer Requests

_____

_____

_____

_____

_____

_____

_____

_____

_____

DAY 10

Exodus 16:8

Also Moses said, "This shall be seen when the Lord gives you meat to eat in the evening, and in the morning bread to the full; for the Lord hears your murmurings which you make against Him. And what are we? Your murmurings are not against us but against the Lord."

I Hate to Complain

Certain expressions in the English language raise doubts in our minds, such as: "Your check is in the mail," from a debtor; "This shouldn't cost much," from your mechanic; or "This won't hurt," from your dentist. Another such expression we often hear is, "I hate to complain." How often have you heard someone say, "I hate to complain, but . . ." and then launch into a lengthy tale of how, in some fashion, you've fallen short of his expectations?

Moses and Aaron heard it a lot. At least on three occasions (at Marah, Ex. 15:24; in the Wilderness of Sin, Ex. 16:2; and at Rephidim, Ex. 17:3), the people complained about the hardships encountered on their journey. In fact, at Rephidim, Moses told God, "The people are ready to stone me!" (17:4).

The truth is, most of us don't mind complaining at all. Yet we need to remember that when we complain, ultimately the person we're finding fault with is God. He is sovereign, so everything that comes into our lives must first meet His approval. When we complain, we are telling God, "You've made a mistake. You shouldn't have allowed this to happen to me." But God is too wise to make a mistake and too loving to permit unnecessary heartache.

When you are next tempted to complain, remember that you have a sovereign God who loves you. All that you experience is to shape and mold you into the best person you can be. Instead of complaining, be happy that God cares enough about you even to allow you hardship under His watchful eye.

Ultimately, all our complaints are directed against God.

Reflections/Prayer Requests

_____

_____

_____

_____

_____

_____

_____

_____

DAY 11

Exodus 16:23

*Then he said to them, "This is what the L*ORD* has said: 'Tomorrow is a Sabbath rest, a holy Sabbath to the L*ORD*. Bake what you will bake today, and boil what you will boil; and lay up for yourselves all that remains, to be kept until morning.'"*

Rest

In 24 hours the average adult accomplishes much: his heart beats 103,689 times, his blood travels 168 million miles, he breathes 23,040 times, he inhales 438 cubic feet of air, he eats 3 1/2 pounds of food and drinks 2.9 quarts of liquid, he speaks 4,800 words, he moves 750 muscles, his nails grow .000046 inch, and he exercises 7 million brain cells. It's no wonder we need rest!

When God established the laws governing the lives of the Israelite people, He built into their schedule a time for rest. Physically it enabled their bodies to recuperate. Spiritually it reminded them that their salvation was not complete. They needed a spiritual "rest" that would come only when the Messiah would take away their sins. The writer of Hebrews makes it clear that even though the Jewish people practiced Sabbath-keeping, the real "rest" was a future event. He declared, "For if

Joshua had given them rest, then He would not afterward have spoken of another day. There remains therefore a rest for the people of God" (Heb. 4:8-9).

In the New Testament the command to "remember the Sabbath day to keep it holy" is the only one of the Ten Commandments not repeated—and for good reason. The spiritual rest that the Old Testament saints looked forward to and which the Sabbath represented is now a reality. Jesus said, "Come to Me, all you who labor and are heavy laden, and I will give you rest" (Matt. 11:28).

Taking a day to rest is still an important part of maintaining a healthy body. But it's a physical necessity, not a spiritual law. Now we can rejoice in the true rest that comes in Christ.

Rest is a matter of wisdom, not law.

Reflections/Prayer Requests

_____

_____

_____

_____

_____

_____

DAY 12

Exodus 17:1-3

Then all the congregation of the children of Israel set out on their journey from the Wilderness of Sin, according to the commandment of the LORD, and camped in Rephidim; but there was no water for the people to drink. Therefore the people contended with Moses, and said, "Give us water, that we may drink." And Moses said to them, "Why do you contend with me? Why do you tempt the LORD?" And the people thirsted there for water, and the people murmured against Moses, and said, "Why is it you have brought us up out of Egypt, to kill us and our children and our livestock with thirst?"

Give 'Em a Brake

Where highway construction is taking place, a sign frequently will be posted that reads, "Give 'Em a Brake." This has a double message: one is to slow down, and the other is to spare the workers from injuries caused by carelessness. Highway workers do their job under hazardous conditions and we need to give them a "brake."

The same sign could have been posted outside the tents of Aaron and Moses. Time after time the people of Israel rushed into judgment against their leaders until finally, here at Rephidim, they were ready to stone Moses to death (v. 4). Only God's intervention prevented a tragedy. Without question, these people needed to give Moses a break.

This sign would fit equally well in front of the homes of many pastors and other church leaders. A study by *Leadership Journal* and Christianity Today, Inc., found that 22.8 percent of pastors have been fired or forced to leave their churches at least once in their career, and one in four of these has experienced this more than once. Sixty-two percent of the discharged pastors said the church that let them go was a "repeat offender" and had fired at least one previous pastor. Isn't it time we gave a break to those called of God to lead His church?

Be very careful when tempted to be critical of your pastor or other church leaders. You may find yourself not only opposing them but God as well. Slow down before passing judgment, sincerely check your motives, and make sure there is a sound, biblical reason for your complaint and not simply a personality issue. More often than not, what you need to do is "give 'em a brake."

Pastors need your grace, not your gripes.

Reflections/Prayer Requests

_____

_____

_____

DAY 13

Exodus 17:5-6

*And the L*ORD *said to Moses, "Go on before the people, and take with you some of the elders of Israel. Also take in your hand your rod with which you struck the river, and go. Behold, I will stand before you there on the rock in Horeb; and you shall strike the rock, and water will come out of it, that the people may drink." And Moses did so in the sight of the elders of Israel.*

Water From the Rock

The importance of water can never be underestimated. Sixty percent of a lean, adult body is composed of water. A person can fast from food for 40 days or longer, but the human body can go only for about 7 days without water even under ideal circumstances.

It's no wonder, then, that the Israelites were getting desperate. The wilderness was far from ideal. It was a hot, desert-like stretch of land dotted with huge rocks but little vegetation. Without water they would quickly perish. So God instructed Moses to strike a rock, and out of this flinty hardness flowed sufficient water to meet the needs of all the people and their livestock.

The Bible writers later saw this rock as a symbol of Christ (1 Cor. 10:4). In the midst of a sin-parched life, Christ offers a well of living water that never runs dry, no matter how often we drink from it.

Have you received Christ as your Savior? If not, trust Jesus today and you will never thirst again. If you want eternal water, come to Jesus who said, "Whoever drinks of the water that I shall give him will never thirst. But the water that I shall give him will become in him a fountain of water springing up into everlasting life" (John 4:14).

The world offers a cistern; Christ offers a well.

Reflections/Prayer Requests

_____

_____

_____

_____

_____

_____

_____

_____

_____

_____

_____

DAY 14

Exodus 17:8

Now Amalek came and fought with Israel in Rephidim.

When Life Isn't Fair

Chris was a young father of four. He had grown up in a Christian home, received Christ as his Savior at a young age, lived a healthy lifestyle and demonstrated a consistent Christian testimony. It was a complete shock when he was diagnosed with cancer. There was no reason for this to happen—except that life isn't fair.

The Israelites also found themselves being treated unfairly. For no apparent reason, a nomadic tribe known as the Amalekites chose to attack them. They had no quarrel with these people, yet for the next several hundred years, off and on, Israel was the object of the Amalekites' hatred and harassment. Life isn't fair.

Fortunately, we have a sovereign God who is able to overrule all circumstances (Rom. 8:28). After three years of treatments, Chris finally recovered. Israel eventually destroyed the Amalekites. Life is not fair, but God is. Sooner or later, God will see that justice is served. It may not be as soon as we would like; it may not be in the way we expect; but God will never be unfair. David declared, "Upon the wicked He will rain coals, fire and brimstone and a burning wind; this shall be the portion of their cup" (Ps. 11:6).

Perhaps you also are experiencing unfair treatment. It might be a coworker who delights in making life difficult for you. It may be a health problem that is keeping you from reaching your fullest potential. Maybe it's an automobile the garage has "fixed" a dozen times, and yet it still doesn't run right. Trust God with your situation. Be patient and let Him work out a solution to your predicament. You may find life unfair, but God never is.

Life is not fair, but God is.

Reflections/Prayer Requests

_____

_____

_____

_____

_____

_____

_____

_____

DAY 15

Exodus 17:9

And Moses said to Joshua, "Choose us some men and go out, fight with Amalek. Tomorrow I will stand on the top of the hill with the rod of God in my hand."

The Mentor

Webster defines a *mentor* as a "trusted counselor or guide." He comes alongside you not to control, but to advise. He is a source of wisdom and counsel. He does not live your life for you, but gently guides you through the potholes and the obstacles so that you can live successfully.

Mentoring may be a new concept for many Christians today, but it's an old idea rooted in biblical tradition. Moses acted as a mentor to Joshua. He advised and trained this young man in all areas of life until, when it was time to receive the mantel of leadership, Joshua was ready.

The Church today needs to return to the practice of mentoring. Paul was a mentor to such young men as Timothy and Titus, whom he called "sons" (1 Tim. 1:2,18; 2 Tim. 2:1; Titus 1:4). To the senior women of the church he commanded, "the older women likewise, that they . . . admonish the young women to love their husbands, to love their children, to be discreet, chaste, homemakers, good, obedient to their own husbands, that the word of God may not be blasphemed" (Titus 2:3-5).

If you are mature in the faith, find someone of the same gender who would be interested in learning from your experiences. If you are a new Christian, seek out the companionship of a believer who demonstrates by the fruit in his life that he has a dynamic relationship with Christ and then seek his counsel. This is God's plan for leadership training. Every Christian should either be mentored or be a mentor.

In helping others, we help ourselves.

Reflections/Prayer Requests

_____

_____

_____

_____

_____

_____

_____

_____

_____

DAY 16

Exodus 17:11-12

And so it was, when Moses held up his hand, that Israel prevailed; and when he let down his hand, Amalek prevailed. But Moses' hands became heavy; so they took a stone and put it under him, and he sat on it. And Aaron and Hur supported his hands, one on one side, and the other on the other side; and his hands were steady until the going down of the sun.

A Little Help From Your Friends

Few things of importance come easy. Noah Webster worked 36 years on his dictionary, while Gibbon labored 26 years on his *Decline and Fall of the Roman Empire*. When Milton was writing *Paradise Lost*, he rose at 4:00 every morning to begin work. Plato wrote the first sentence of the *Republic* nine times before it was acceptable to him.

In the midst of challenging circumstances, it's wonderful to have friends who will come along and give their help. Moses experienced such a blessing. The conflict with the Amalekites was a key battle. If the Israelites were defeated at such an early stage on their journey, they likely would become so discouraged that they would turn around and go back to Egypt. Victory was essential, but it wouldn't come easy. The Israelites were winning only when Moses held up his hands in prayer. After hours in this position, however, his arms began to tire and defeat seemed a real possibility. That was when Aaron and Hur stepped in. With a little help from his friends, Moses was able to keep his hands held up until the enemy was thoroughly defeated.

Prayer is the key to victory, but it's also hard work. Often our spirits, if not our hands, grow weary and we face the potential of defeat. That's when we need other believers like Aaron and Hur to step in and lend their strength to our efforts. Praying with friends gives us renewed vigor.

Be sensitive to the opportunities to respond as Aaron and Hur did. Maybe there is someone today who needs you to lend your prayers to his efforts. God will lead you to that person; just make yourself available. Your strength may be essential for his victory.

Victory is never won alone.

Reflections/Prayer Requests

_____

_____

_____

_____

DAY 17

Write It Down

Have you noticed how prone to forget we humans are? Abraham Lincoln observed about his own generation, "We have been the recipients of the choicest bounties of heaven. We have grown in numbers, wealth, and power, as no other nation has ever grown. But we have forgotten God. We have forgotten the gracious hand which preserved us in peace and which multiplied, and enriched, and strengthened us."

God recognized that people have the habit of forgetting, so He instructed Moses to write down in a book what had taken place in the battle against the Amalekites. Furthermore, this was to be read to Joshua, the future leader of Israel, so he would be sure to remember as well. This victory would become a source of encouragement for Christians throughout history—all because it was written down.

Are you keeping a written account of the good things God has done for you? Is there a record of the victories that God has brought about in your life? Some people keep a daily spiritual diary; others record only special events. But in some fashion God's blessings need to be committed to something more dependable than our faulty memories.

When you're feeling discouraged, or perhaps even wondering if God loves you, take out your journal and refresh your memory. The entries in your journal can be a continuing source of encouragement for you. In addition, take the opportunity to share with your children or grandchildren what God has done for you. The God who has dealt with you so graciously in the past is the same God who wants to work in their lives as well.

The weakest ink is stronger than the greatest memory.

Reflections/Prayer Requests

_____

_____

_____

_____

_____

_____

_____

_____

DAY 18

Exodus 17:15-16

And Moses built an altar and called its name, The-LORD-Is-My-Banner; for he said, "Because the LORD has sworn: the LORD will have war with Amalek from generation to generation."

His Banner Over Me

Queen Elizabeth II of England has three royal residences (Buckingham Palace, Windsor Castle and the Palace of Holyrood) plus two private homes. This could be confusing for those who want to find her except for one important fact: the queen's banner always flies over whichever residence she is currently occupying. If her banner of blue and gold is on the flagpole, the queen is sure to be present.

Moses also had a banner. After the battle with the army of Amalek, he built an altar and called it "The-LORD-Is-My-Banner." Moses wanted everyone to know that God was in residence with His people. Despite the attacks of the Amalekites, God would never desert the people of Israel. Generation after generation could look up and know that the Lord was present in their midst.

As Christians, we should raise the Lord's banner over our lives. No matter how difficult our situation becomes, God will not abandon His residence in our midst. The apostle John declared, "And the Word became flesh and dwelt among us" (John 1:14). And Jesus said, "I am with you always, even to the end of the age" (Matt. 28:20). If the King is present, His banner should fly.

Is it obvious to those around you that the King is in residence in your life? Make sure that His flag, colored with faith, hope and love, flies high over the castle of your life. It's a privilege to fly that banner; it's a shame not to.

If the King is in residence, be sure to fly His flag.

Reflections/Prayer Requests

DAY 19

Exodus 18:2-5

Then Jethro, Moses' father-in-law, took Zipporah, Moses' wife, after he had sent her back, with her two sons, of whom the name of one was Gershom . . . and the name of the other was Eliezer . . . and Jethro, Moses' father-in-law, came with his sons and his wife to Moses in the wilderness, where he was encamped at the mountain of God.

A Family Reunion

Beau Arceneaux was 15 months old when he was kidnapped by his father and taken from Louisiana to live in Austin, Texas. Years later, as he visited a chat room on the Internet, a couple of people became curious about this boy who had no contact with his mother. So they informed the police. In December 1995, the FBI showed up at Beau's home to tell him his mother had been searching for him for the past 12 years. On December 20, mother and son were joyfully reunited.

Have you ever been separated from your family? If you have ever been apart from your family for any length of time, you know how difficult it is. I was apart from my wife and children during my last semester of seminary while I was studying in France. I was thousands of miles away, living in a foreign country, knowing I would not see them for months. It wasn't easy.

Moses also had been separated from his family. Zipporah, his wife of 40 years, and his two sons had been sent back to the land of Midian while he returned to Egypt to lead Israel to freedom. With that challenge behind him, Moses was ready to be reunited with his loved ones—and Jethro was gracious enough to bring this about. While Scripture gives no details, you can imagine what a joyful reunion it was.

As Christians we also have the joy of anticipating a very special reunion. Scripture says, "And the dead in Christ will rise first. Then we who are alive and remain shall be caught up together with them in the clouds to meet the Lord in the air. And thus we shall always be with the Lord" (1 Thess. 4:16-17). Now that's a family reunion! Someday we'll experience a reunion that never ends. Hallelujah!

Christians never say "good-bye"; just "until we meet again."

Reflections/Prayer Requests

_____

_____

_____

_____

DAY 20

Exodus 18:7-8

So Moses went out to meet his father-in-law, bowed down, and kissed him. And they asked each other about their well-being, and they went into the tent. And Moses told his father-in-law all that the Lord had done to Pharaoh and to the Egyptians for Israel's sake, all the hardship that had come upon them on the way, and how the LORD had delivered them.

Respecting Your Elders

Rodney Dangerfield is the original "I don't get no respect" man. No matter how hard he tries, to hear the comedian tell it, no one shows him any respect. Some of the elderly could voice the same complaint. As more people are living longer, they are becoming the victims of everything from physical abuse to con artists' scams.

This differs significantly from the respect Moses showed his father-in-law. Even though Moses was the leader of a great host of people, he bowed before Jethro as a sign of humility and kissed him as a sign of affection. And in the midst of the many needs of a demanding people, he took time to share with Jethro all the events that had transpired since he had seen him last.

As we deal with the elderly, we must do so with patience and compassion. Most of them

42

have made significant sacrifices to raise their families, to defend their country and to make an honest living. In their golden years they deserve to be treated with respect.

If you have elderly parents, take time to be involved in their lives. Listen to their stories (even if you've heard then a hundred times before); sympathize with their aches and pains; look for opportunities to make their lives a little easier. If your parents are no longer alive, perhaps there is an elderly neighbor or someone at church who could benefit from your attention. We are not judged by how we treat the strong and powerful but by how we respect the weak and helpless. Besides, having made an investment of time and interest in an elderly person, you may discover that the return on your investment was greater than the investment itself.

Treat the elderly as a nonrenewable resource; they are!

Reflections/Prayer Requests

_____

_____

_____

_____

_____

DAY 21

And Jethro said, "Blessed be the LORD, who has delivered you out of the hand of the Egyptians and out of the hand of Pharaoh, and who has delivered the people from under the hand of the Egyptians. Now I know that the LORD is greater than all the gods; for in the very thing in which they behaved proudly, He was above them."

Great Is the Lord

Soviet Premier Nikita Khrushchev once boasted that he would display the last Soviet Christian on television by 1965. Khrushchev is long dead; Christianity is more alive than ever in Russia. Karl Marx called a belief in God "the sign of the oppressed creature, the opium of the people." Marx also has gone to his eternal destiny, but the "opium" he spoke of continues to spread throughout the world. And so it has been. Leaders rise up, shake their fists at God, and then sink back into the oblivion from which they came. In the meantime, God continues to work out His plan for the world, undisturbed by their puny efforts against Him.

Jethro, Moses' father-in-law, observed the same truth about Pharaoh and the gods of Egypt. Arrogantly they had shaken their fists at God, but "He was above them." Like an ant trying to stop a locomotive, they challenged the Almighty and lost. Once again God proved "that the Lord is greater than all the gods."

Throughout history, God has demonstrated that He is greater than any person, any movement, or any situation. It is obvious why the psalmist could confidently boast, "I will lift up my eyes to the hills—from whence comes my help? My help comes from the LORD, who made heaven and earth" (Ps. 121:1). God Himself declares, "Behold, I am the LORD, the God of all flesh. Is there anything too hard for Me?" (Jer. 32:27).

If you are fearful about some godless person, some anti-Christian movement, or some threatening situation, remember where your help comes from. The God who is above all other gods will never be overwhelmed by your difficulties. The God who delivered Moses will deliver you as well. He's just that kind of God.

Trouble never troubles God.

Reflections/Prayer Requests

_____

_____

_____

DAY 22

Exodus 18:14, 17

*So when Moses' father-in-law saw all that he did
for the people, he said, "What is this thing that
you are doing for the people? Why do you alone
sit, and all the people stand before you
from morning until evening?"
So Moses' father-in-law said to him,
"The thing that you do is not good."*

The Test of a True Friend

Antisthenes, the cynic philosopher, use to
say, "There are only two people who will tell
you the truth about yourself—an enemy who
has lost his temper and a friend who loves
you dearly." The true test of a friend is not
how frequently he is with you but how honest
he is with you.

Jethro, Moses' father-in-law, was a true
friend. When he saw Moses wearing himself
out doing something that others could do just
as well, he plainly said, "The thing that you do
is not good." His concern for his son-in-law's
health would not allow him to stay quiet.

Telling our friends the truth has its hazards
because the truth often hurts. Their initial
reaction may not be a positive one. Yet
Scripture says, "Faithful are the wounds of a
friend, but the kisses of an enemy are deceit-
ful" (Prov. 27:6). The role of a faithful friend is
not always an easy one.

If you find it necessary to share a potentially hurtful truth with your friend, approach the situation only after much prayer. Pray that your attitude would be one of humility and servanthood. Ask God to provide the right situation in which to share the truth. Seek wisdom in how to best express yourself so that what you say will be viewed by your friend as constructive rather than destructive. Pray, prepare, then just do it. Faithfulness is not gauged by your intentions but by your actions. You never help your friend with good intentions alone, but with good intentions that result in good actions.

A faithful friend is a truthful friend.

Reflections/Prayer Requests

DAY 23

Exodus 18:21

Moreover you shall select from all the people able men, such as fear God, men of truth, hating covetousness; and place such over them to be rulers of thousands, rulers of hundreds, rulers of fifties, and rulers of tens.

Looking for Leadership

In 1789 an uncertain George Washington was urged to seek the presidency by Governor Morris, a Pennsylvania delegate to the Constitutional Convention. Morris wrote Washington, "No constitution is the same on paper and in life. The exercise of authority depends upon personal character."

Jethro, Moses' father-in-law, recognized this truth as well. He knew that his plan to relieve some of the stress in his son-in-law's life depended on the character of the men who were chosen to execute it. That's why he urged Moses to choose men who were not only competent but who also had a healthy fear of God, who spoke the truth and avoided greed.

Unfortunately, this fundamental principle of public service is often not carefully observed. In both church and government, people have been put into positions of leadership based on their abilities with little regard for their character. In fact, one poll found that 67 percent of voters think a political leader can have "substantial flaws in personal character" but still govern effectively. Such a position is contrary to Scripture, experience, and common sense.

As you face the responsibility of electing officials in your church and government, give careful consideration to their character. Select individuals who not only are able, but who also fear God, uphold the truth and reject greed. People of good character who possess no skills in leadership usually do not make good leaders. But people with leadership skills and little character make even worse leaders. They lead us wherever their character will permit, and that is usually not toward God.

What a man is will always determine what a man does.

Reflections/Prayer Requests

_____

_____

_____

_____

_____

_____

DAY 24

Exodus 18:22

And let them judge the people at all times. Then it will be that every great matter they shall bring to you, but every small matter they themselves shall judge. So it will be easier for you, for they will bear the burden with you.

Burden Bearers

Andrew C. Davison wrote about an encounter with Dr. Albert Schweitzer at Lambarene, on the banks of the Ogowe River. It was about noon and the sun was beating down mercilessly as a group walked up a hill with Dr. Schweitzer. Suddenly the doctor strode across the slope to where an African woman was struggling with a load of wood for the cooking fires. The 85-year-old doctor took the entire burden and carried it up the hill for the relieved woman. When they reached the top of the hill, someone asked Dr. Schweitzer why he did things like that, implying that in that heat and at his age he should not. Albert Schweitzer pointed to the woman and said simply, "No one should have to carry a burden like that alone."

That was Moses' problem—he was trying to carry his burden alone. It took the wise insight of his father-in-law, Jethro, to point out the fact that others "will bear the burden with you."

God's people were never meant to carry their burdens alone. That's why we have the privilege of prayer. Peter urged us to cast "all your care upon Him, for He cares for you" (1 Pet. 5:7). Bearing burdens is also the role of the Church. Paul instructed believers, "Bear one another's burdens, and so fulfill the law of Christ" (Gal. 6:2).

Are you willing to help others bear their burdens? Perhaps even today there is someone who needs you to pray with him, cook a meal or provide transportation for him. It's not hard to spot burdens that need to be borne when you are looking for them. Our responsibility is to do whatever it takes to make a burden lighter. That's a responsibility that brings great satisfaction now and eternal reward in the future.

A burden shared is a lighter load.

Reflections/Prayer Requests

_____

_____

_____

_____

_____

_____

_____

DAY 25

Exodus 19:3-4

And Moses went up to God, and the L<small>ORD</small> called to him from the mountain, saying, "Thus you shall say to the house of Jacob, and tell the children of Israel: 'You have seen what I did to the Egyptians, and how I bore you on eagles' wings and brought you to Myself.'"

No Obstacles Allowed

A friend told me that when he was a young boy, he lived on one side of his small town and the school he attended was located on the other. Bus transportation was limited to the students who lived out of the city limit, so he had to walk many blocks both to and from school. "After a tiring day at school," my friend explained, "I would sometimes fantasize on my way home of having wings that would lift me over all the houses and trees and deposit me directly on my front porch."

It was wings like these that God figuratively used to bring Israel to Himself. In spite of the obstruction of Pharaoh and his army, through the barrier of a seemingly uncrossable sea, over the hurdle of a dry and barren wilderness, God lifted His people up and brought them safely to their destination. No obstacle was allowed to stand between Him and those He loved.

Are you facing obstacles today that threaten your joy as a Christian? Maybe these obstacles are health problems, financial struggles or family relationships. Perhaps you are frustrated by circumstances beyond your control. Well, don't fantasize as my friend did. Instead, look to God's mighty wings to lift you up and carry you to where He wants you to be. Remember the promise of Isaiah 40:31: "But those who wait on the Lord shall renew their strength; they shall mount up with wings like eagles, they shall run and not be weary, they shall walk and not faint." Claim that promise today.

What you can't go through, God will help you fly over.

Reflections/Prayer Requests

_____

_____

_____

_____

_____

_____

_____

_____

DAY 26

Exodus 19:9

And the LORD said to Moses, "Behold, I come to you in the thick cloud, that the people may hear when I speak with you, and believe you forever." So Moses told the words of the people to the LORD.

No Room for Doubt

A popular definition of faith is "believing something without proof." Someone else said that faith "is believing something you know isn't true." Yet neither of these is the kind of faith the Bible talks about.

When God prepared to speak to Moses, He came in a thick cloud—something that would be obvious to everyone. This was not for God's benefit; He chose to manifest Himself in this way so that everyone would have undeniable proof that He truly had spoken to Moses and they would believe him forever.

Throughout history, God has left a record of these undeniable proofs. No one needs to take the Christian faith merely on the basis that "someone says so." Instead, God has provided such evidence as changed lives, the inerrant Word and, most important, the empty tomb. The apostle John wrote near the end of his Gospel: "And truly Jesus did many other signs in the presence of His disciples, which are not written in this book; but these are written that you may believe that Jesus is the Christ, the Son of God, and that believing you may have life in His name" (John 20:30-31). And Luke wrote near the beginning of the Acts that Jesus "presented Himself alive after His suffering by many infallible proofs" (Acts 1:3).

During those times when doubts arise, quench them with a healthy dose of proof. Read your Bible and you'll be filled with confidence. God doesn't ask us to take a leap into the unknown. Instead, He says, "Come now, and let us reason together" (Isa. 1:18). Don't be afraid to take God up on His offer. He will leave no room for doubt.

Our faith is based on facts, not fiction.

Reflections/Prayer Requests

_____
_____
_____
_____
_____
_____
_____
_____

DAY 27

Exodus 19:10-11

Then the LORD said to Moses, "Go to the people and sanctify them today and tomorrow, and let them wash their clothes. And let them be ready for the third day. For on the third day the LORD will come down upon Mount Sinai in the sight of all the people."

The God Who Is Near

A supposedly true story tells that a very rich man in London died and left a large gift to one of the hospitals there. His will stipulated, however, that as a condition for the gift, his ashes were to be brought to the board room for each board meeting and placed at the head of the table. Accordingly, for more than 100 years the secretary of the board added these words to the minutes of each meeting: "Jeremy Benthan, present but not voting."

While this ongoing request may seem a bit ludicrous to you and me, the God of Israel also desired to be present with His people, and that wasn't ludicrous at all. As they prepared to receive His law, He came down upon Mount Sinai in such a way that everyone knew He was present in their midst. In a very visible manner, God demonstrated His desire to have fellowship with His people.

John made the same observation about Jesus. When it was time to redeem the human race, the apostle said, "And the Word became flesh and dwelt among us" (John 1:14). Jesus promised, "For where two or three are gathered together in My name, I am there in the midst of them" (Matt. 18:20). And again He said, "I am with you always, even to the end of the age" (Matt. 28:20).

Do you see the evidences of God's presence in your life? Have you felt the warmth of His presence, the gentleness of His touch or the strength of His everlasting arms? Take both joy and comfort in knowing that you have a God who not only loves you but also wants to be with you.

When you put your hand in God's hand, you will never walk alone.

Reflections/Prayer Requests

DAY 28

Exodus 20:1-3

And God spoke all these words, saying: "I am the LORD your God, who brought you out of the land of Egypt, out of the house of bondage. You shall have no other gods before Me."

Priority One

John Wanamaker was a man who had his priorities straight. In the late 19th century he opened a department store in Philadelphia. Within a few years the enterprise became one of the most successful businesses in the country. But operating his store wasn't Wanamaker's only responsibility. He was also named Postmaster General of the United States and served as the superintendent for what was then the largest Sunday school in the world at Bethany Presbyterian Church. When someone asked him how he could hold all these positions at once, he explained, "Early in life I read, 'But seek first the kingdom of God and His righteousness, and all these things shall be added to you' [Matt. 6:33]. That's what I've done." In the midst of a busy life, Mr. Wanamaker made God his number-one priority and the results speak for themselves.

As the Israelites began their new life of freedom, God instructed them to "have no

58

other gods before Me." This was not for His benefit, but for theirs. To live life successfully, we must know what's most important. All of our other priorities will be out of kilter until we get our first priority straight. When we know what comes first, the rest will fall into place. God must always come first in our lives, in our daily schedules, our checkbooks, our estate plans, our thoughts and our actions. He is priority one.

If your life is chaotic, it may indicate your priorities are jumbled. Make God priority one in your life and you may be surprised at how easily everything else comes together. Only by starting your priorities right can you hope to end them right.

Everything begins with the right priorities, and right priorities begin with God.

Reflections/Prayer Requests

_____

_____

_____

_____

_____

_____

_____

DAY 29

Honor Your Parents

On her 80th birthday, a woman from Brooklyn decided to prepare her last will and testament. She went to her pastor to make two final requests. First, she insisted on cremation.

"What is your second request?" the pastor asked.

"I want my ashes scattered over Bloomingdale's."

"Why Bloomingdale's?"

"Then I'll be sure that my daughters will visit me twice a week."

Unfortunately, there's a lot of truth in that humor. In Japan, for instance, a company is offering actors to play the part of family members. The actors will visit elderly parents as surrogates for the real family members. In Oakland, California, a 62-year-old man who could neither walk nor talk was found abandoned on a flight from El Paso, Texas. A note was pinned to his clothing saying he needed medical attention.

Such disregard for one's parents is directly contrary to God's instructions. He exhorts us to show respect and concern for our parents and even attaches promises of longevity for those willing to obey.

As life becomes crowded with a multitude of commitments—at school, at church and at home—don't forget that the ones who gave you life may now require your attention as well. Check to see if they have needs that are going unmet; if they live close by, invite them to join you in your family's activities. Most of all, demonstrate your love and respect for them by simply taking time to be with them and listen to them. If you can't do that, pick up the telephone and call them often. Let them talk as long as they want. Their days may not be long now, but God promises that your days will be long upon the land if you honor your father and mother. Don't allow this treasure to pass by your life unenjoyed.

Honor your parents and the Lord will honor you.

Reflections/Prayer Requests

_____

_____

_____

_____

DAY 30

Exodus 20:13

You shall not murder.

Respect for Life

Every 22 seconds someone in the United States is beaten, stabbed, shot, robbed, raped or killed. The average American citizen has a 1 in 153 chance of being murdered. Intentional killings—murders and suicides—rank fourth among causes of U.S. deaths, after heart disease, cancer and accidents. Obviously, such a low regard for human life is appalling and reflects how far America has strayed from the principles of the Ten Commandments.

But Jesus broadened the "You shall not murder" commandment even more. He said, "You have heard that it was said to those of old, 'You shall not murder, and whoever murders will be in danger of the judgment.' But I say to you that whoever is angry with his brother without a cause shall be in danger of the judgment" (Matt. 5:21-22).

While Christians are unlikely to murder someone physically, they can easily be murderers in their heart. Perhaps you can identify with Clarence Darrow, the famous criminal lawyer, who said, "Everyone is a potential murderer. I have not killed anyone, but I frequently get satisfaction out of obituary notices."

When we have hatred in our hearts toward someone or we nurse an angry attitude toward a person who has offended us, we qualify under Jesus' guidelines as murderers. That may be shocking, but it's true. If you fall into this category, ask God to forgive you and to replace your anger and bitterness with an unconditional love for the one you previously hated. Go to that person and seek reconciliation. Ask for forgiveness because of your inappropriate attitudes. Reach out to her and try to make your one-time enemy your friend. It's the only way to remove murderous attitudes from your heart. Since your attitudes are just as important as your actions, don't dismiss too quickly what the Lord Jesus said. Take an attitude check today and see if there is murder in your heart, even if it is not in your head.

An attitude can murder just as easily as an ax.

Reflections/Prayer Requests

_____

_____

_____

_____

DAY 31

Exodus 20:14

You shall not commit adultery.

An Undefiled Bed

A newspaper publisher offered a prize for the best answer to the question, "Why is a newspaper like a good woman?" The winning answer was, "Because every man should have one of his own and not look at his neighbor's!"

While the publisher's contest may not have been in the best of taste, the winning answer certainly contains an important truth. As the Israelites moved out into pagan nations that worshiped fertility gods and goddesses, God knew they would face strong temptations to sexual immorality. Therefore He bluntly commanded them, "You shall not commit adultery."

This same command is repeated in a number of ways in the New Testament. The writer of Hebrews says, "Marriage is honorable among all, and the bed undefiled; but fornicators and adulterers God will judge" (Heb. 13:4). The apostle Paul ranks adultery on the same level as idolatry, sorcery, murder, and drunkenness, among other sins of the flesh (Gal. 5:19-21). We must also remember that Jesus expanded the meaning of adultery beyond the physical act to include lusting in our hearts (Matt. 5:27-28). In fact, almost all adultery begins in the heart.

In our own day, when adultery and almost every other form of sexual immorality is accepted as commonplace, Christians need to walk carefully as well. Satan will use everything including the scantily clad person on the beach, the pornographic magazines sold at the local gas station or the suggestive shows on television to cause you to stumble.

If you struggle with sexual temptation, begin to memorize God's Word, especially verses that talk about purity (such as Matt. 5:8 and 1 Tim. 5:22). If the problem begins in the heart, hide God's Word there so you can nip temptation at the point of origin (Ps. 119:11). Share your struggle with a trusted friend who can both keep your confidence and keep you accountable. Whatever it might cost in terms of wounded pride and denied desires, it will be worth it all.

When adultery walks in, everything worth having walks out.

Reflections/Prayer Requests

_____

_____

_____